Additional Praise for *The War Still Within*

Dedicated in part to her long-dead mother and to women who have lost their names, Tanya Ko Hong's *The War Still Within* wages its battles in one exquisitely revealing poem after another. The author gives names to the nameless: the Korean comfort women during WWII, as well as women who came after, women who suffered too long in silence, whose sad fate shackled them to lives of quiet desperation. This extraordinary book is for them, and for all of us.

> —Alexis Rhone Fancher, poetry editor of *Cultural Weekly* and
>   author of five books of poetry

The compressed, intense, emotionally chilling poem "Comfort Woman" impressed me greatly and...has moved to tears many of those who have read or heard it.

> —John Rosenwald, poet, translator, professor emeritus, and
>   co-editor of *Beloit Poetry Journal* from 2002 to 2016

Great injustices are difficult to render in small literary spaces, but Tanya Ko finds the right tone—sensitive, intimate, yet restrained. In sparse, precise scenes, "Comfort Woman" both informs and moves us in unforgettable ways.

> —Leonore Hildebrandt, Creative Writing faculty, University of Maine

In *The War Still Within*, Tanya Ko Hong illuminates dark corners of forbidden territories. She exposes her own history and struggles as a Korean-American woman, and in a searingly frank sequence she writes in the voices of those who were Korean "comfort women" during WWII. She delicately balances a stance that is explicit as well as gorgeously reflective. She vivifies and deepens experience in this dynamic collection. We should follow her lead, follow her call as a way into the future: "Tonight my tongue cuts galaxy."

> —Molly Bendall, author of five books of poetry and professor
>   of English at USC Dornsife (University of Southern California)

Also by Tanya Ko Hong (Hyonhye)

Mother to Myself
A collection of poems in Korean
(Purunsasang, 2015)

Yellow Flowers on a Rainy Day
(Oma Books of the Pacific, 2003)

Mother's Diary from Generation 1.5
(Korean edition: Qumran Publishing, 2002)

Generation 1.5
(Korea: Esprit Books, 1993)

Table of Contents

Dedicated to my mother,
Jae Yoon Yu (1936–1995):
the life she lived, without ever
seeing her grandchildren

And to my daughter,
Soolgi Hong (b. 1996):
the life she is living

And for all the women everywhere
who have lost their names

The Way to Cross the Desert

Do not think about
the oasis.

✧

Gacela of Moonshine

I want to dance like her on the crowded floor
I want to writhe in music guiltless as a child
I want eternal blood circulating like a halo
I want to dance like a rising sun in Death Valley

I do not want to live like a shadow
I refuse to numb my dragon heart
I do not want to please like a lotus on a pond
I refuse to remain a fingerprint on your thigh

Remember the dancing ends at midnight
the red snake may bite your neck
while your pomegranate cheeks still burn
and you might never get home

I want to keep dancing
dance through the war, generations of dark matter
the flame of my feet will burn through
I'll dance like a raven on a sand dune

Waiting

When I think of you, rain comes
When I call you, you come in rain
When I touch you, you disappear

in rain

Bring me raw garlic and a handful
of bitter green wormwood
I will eat them and stay in a cave
21 days, 100 days
That's how bear became woman
I will do the same—
    if I can see you one last time

There is another myth:
when you fold one thousand paper cranes
your dream comes true
If I can see you one last time
I will fold thousands—
    ten thousand paper cranes

I want to open your apartment door again
with the key that you sent by mail
the key still warm from your hand
I want to hang my clothes in your closet
between your clothes—
    I want to feel safe there again

Waiting for you is nothing
Without blinking, I watch
the night become silver rain in blue light

I will wait for you like a rock on the water line
wishing you to be a wave and reach me
If you touch
I will collapse and be water like you

✧

Bo go ship uh (I miss you)

I miss you
is not enough

bo go ship uh
no subject

puffy eyes with red veins
praying before sunlight
putting away a fresh bowl of rice
between blankets to keep warm

waiting
contains silence
sorrow

could not touch
through DMZ
the divided country

husband in the North
wife in the South
child in her belly

Comfort Woman

14 August 1991, Seoul, South Korea:

A woman named Hak Soon Kim [Kim Hak-Sun, 1924–1997] came forward to denounce the Japanese for the sexual enslavement of more than 200,000 women during World War II. They were known as "Wianbu" in Korean and "Comfort Women" in English.

1991, Seoul, South Korea

The voice on TV is comforting,
like having a person beside me
talking all the time
while I eat my burnt rice gruel.

Suddenly in Japanese:
But we didn't—
Those women came to us
for the money.
We never forced—
I dropped
my spoon into my *nureun bap.*

On the screen
a photograph of young girls
seated in an open truck
like the one I rode with Soonja
over the rice-field road years ago.

3 a.m.
Waking in a cold sweat
I gulp *Jariki*
bul kuk
bul kuk
but my throat still burns.

I reach for a cigarette
and the white smoke spirals
like Soonja's wandering soul...

They called me *wianbu—*
a comfort woman—
but I had a name.

1939, Chinju, South Kyangsan Province

We are going to do Senninbari, right?
No, Choingsindae, Women's Labor Corps.
Same thing, right?
Earn money
become new woman
come back home soon—

Holding tiny hands
fingertips
bong soong ah
balsam-flower red
colored by summer's end

Ripening persimmons
bending over the Choga roofs
fade into distance

When the truck crosses the last hill
leaving our hometown in the dust
Soonja kicks off her white shoes

1941, That Autumn

Autumn night, Japanese
soldiers wielding swords
dragged me away
while I was gathering pine needles

that fell from my basket
filling the air with the scent
of their white blood

When you scream in your dream
there's no sound

On the *maru*, Grandma's making *Songpyeon*,
asking Mom, *Is the water boiling?*
Will she bring pine needles before
my eyeballs fall out?

I feel pain
there—

They put a long stick between my legs—
Open up, open, Baka Chosengjing!
they rage, spraying
their sperm
the smell of
burning dog
burning life

panting
grunting on top of me

Under my blood I am dying

1943, Shanghai, China

One night
a soldier asked all the girls

Who can do one hundred men?

I raised my hand
Soonja did not

The soldiers put her in boiling water
alive
and fed us

What is living?

Is Soonja living in me?

1946, Chinju, Korea

One year after
liberation
I came home

Short hair
not wearing *hanbok*
not speaking clearly

Mother hid me
in the back room
At night she took me to the well
and washed me
Scars seared with hot steel
like burnt bark
like roots of old trees
all over my body

Under the crescent glow
she smiled when she washed me
My baby! Your skin is like white jade, dazzling
She bit her lower lip
washing my belly softly
but they had ripped open my womb
with the baby inside

Mother made white rice and seaweed soup
put my favorite white fish on top
But Mother, I can't eat flesh

That night in the granary
she hanged herself
left a little bag in my room
my dowry, with a rice ball

Father threw it at me
waved his hand toward the door

I left at dusk

30 years

40 years

forever

Mute
mute
mute

bury it with me

They called me wianbu—
I had a name

1991, 3:00 AM

(That night
the thousand blue stars
became white butterflies
through ripped rice paper
and flew into my room

One
One hundred
One thousand butterflies—

Endless white butterflies going through
the web in my mouth
into my unhealed red scars
stitching one by one
butterflies lifting me
    heavier than the dead
butterflies opening my bedroom door
        heavier than shame)

At
dawn,
I stand.

Footnotes:

1. *Baka Chosengjing*: a derogatory term translated loosely as "stupid Korean" and conveying contempt for a culture the soldiers despised
2. *bong soong ah*: a traditional Korean plant dye made from the Garden Balsam flower, used to color fingernails and fingertips
3. *Jariki*: drinking water placed at bedside
4. *maru*: traditional Korean floor made of wood
5. *nureun bap*: scorched rice re-boiled with water
6. *Songpyeon*: traditional Korean rice cake for *Chusuk* holiday

✧

Grandmother Talks of Camptowns

At 77 years old all my teeth are gone
and the wind blows past my gums.
No windscreen here in Dongducheon
where homeless live alone.

Rather than live alone
I wanted to be a monk in Buddha's temple
but they kicked me out—
I sneaked the bacon.

The Deacon's ad in the newspaper
offered a room at his church.
In exchange for cleaning I lived well.
One rainy night I drank *soju* and smoked—
so they kicked me out.

Damn hard work on my back for GIs—
pounded and pounded me inside
so one day it had to go.
The *khanho-won* removed my womb.
No pension, no *yungkum*
for sex trade.

American couple adopted
my half-white son—
my half-black daughter
I left at the orphanage door
and never knew her fate.

At one time I had money saved.
My brother came with his guilty face:
Because I can't protect you, you do this.
He used my handling money
to become a lawyer and soon removed
my name from the family—like scraping
a baby from the womb.

Still, on my birthdays my sister Sook
secretly came to see me,
came with seaweed soup.
Unni, Unni...
I waited for her to come,
saved a gift chocolate so carefully wrapped,
gum, perfume, Dove soap...

Now that she's engaged
Sook cannot come again.
Why can't you go to America like the others?
For the first time that day I was weeping,
Mother, Mother, we should not live—
let's die together!—but Mother was already gone.

The time goes so fast that people on the moon
didn't know where Korea was.

One day I met a man
and I was a woman making rice,
washing his work clothes, submissive
and joyful until he found my American dollars,
ran away and never came back.

Now in Dongducheon
look—
stars shimmer in the wind.

Footnotes:

1. *khanho-won*: nurse
2. *Unni*: a term of respect and endearment for an older sister

✧

Suk Su Dong

Suk means rock, Su means water, and Dong means town.
Water comes down from the mountains where
temples hide in the forests.
Grey-gowned monks chant ghost secrets,
tap *moktak* at dawn.

Kun Sunim, Big Monk, shaved her head,
hid her breasts in robes and had a son.
She rented out rooms in the temple,
put meat in her dumplings—even pork—
but everybody bowed *hop jang* as she passed.

Near mountain temples, statues
of men and women offer their genitals
to childless couples. People come
to bow, touch statues' *songgi*, and wait
for life to grow.

Footnote:

hop jang: with hands pressed together

A Blonde Whispers Korean in My Ear

We were drinking homemade wine
at a child's birthday party
when a blonde mom told me:

Once I had a Korean boyfriend.
His mother hated me
but how I loved her
food, Bulgogi, Japchae,
and you know you can't kiss
after you eat that—
what's it called?—the smelly cabbage
made with salted baby shrimp,
anchovy, garlic, chili...

She giggled.

I know a bad Korean word, she said.

Whisper in my ear, I said.

Jajee.

Her face bloomed red as *bong soong ah.*
My face was a frozen trout.

Only a whore uses that word.
Never wives—not even to their husbands.
Never moms—not in front of the children.

When referring to the penis, a Korean doctor says
songgi, a Chinese word—
even after Koreans invented it.

That's not a bad word, I replied.
It's just a part of the body.

Who does she think she is to say that word?
When I've never pronounced it with *my* mouth.

Author's note:

As an immigrant of the Korean diaspora, I know what it feels like being invisible, voiceless, and powerless. Writing poems has been a long process: even allowing myself to write certain words felt like an impossible transgression. At times I was sick at heart, in pain and angry, but something magical was happening. I was able to expose my own wounds through new symbols and images.

—From *Rattle* (Issue 59, Spring 2018), "Tribute to Immigrant Poets"

Footnote:

bong soong ah: a traditional Korean plant dye made from the Garden Balsam flower, used to color fingernails and fingertips

The Dal Rae River

A Korean folktale

It was a rainy day
when the brother and sister went over the mountain
She walked in front and he followed

Rain soaked my summer clothing
revealed the shape
of nipples, thighs, hips

You saw in me
a woman
Not your sister

It was a rainy day
He followed over the mountain

They'll need a story to make you a hero
They'll need a tiger or something
You'll need a scar across your chest

Hurt me to prove
I was almost
killed

My son, my brave son
fought the tiger
and saved his useless sister

Oh, brother, *dal rae na bo jee, dal rae na bo jee*

Why did you do that?
Mother and Father will send me away
I am the worthless

They won't let me come into the house
They will live with regrets
I will never be seen

It was a rainy day
when the brother and sister went over the mountain
She walked in front and he followed…

You were hitting your cock with stone
You hung yourself to tree and gore

Oh, brother,
dal rae na bo jee, dal rae na bo jee,
why didn't you ask me?

I would have given myself
to you

Tiki Boy

Johnny was white-boy pretty:
pale skin and soft gold hair
that shone even more in the sun,

his eyes
blue glass marbles
reflecting me.

Old people in our town pointed
and called him *tiki*,
the mixed child,
but never in front of his mother,

her face powdered white as dog bone.
The women said, *You're so pretty—*
but when she wasn't there:
That Yang kalbo,
her lips look
like she's eaten mice.

Her long false eyelashes could hold match sticks
under her Crayola sapphire eyelids.

Johnny's big-nosed GI daddy
wore black-frame eyeglasses.

Johnny would climb
over the wall topped with
broken glass and
we plucked the honeysuckle,
sipped the nectar
we loved
more than Ritz Crackers and milk.

One day he said, "An airplane will take me away
to America,"
then pointed at the sky and played
his lip like a kazoo.

I replied that I'd rather take a bus or train.

When I saw him again,
years later in Honolulu, sitting
alone with a beer,
he wore
glasses like his father's.

When I said "hi" to him
in Korean,
he said, "I don't remember Korea."

Still, I remember
the sweet honeysuckle
we plucked
and sipping the nectar
we loved more than Ritz Crackers and milk.

Footnote:

Yang kalbo: Yankee's prostitute; also, Western whore

✧

Oxtail Soup

I look at the *mung* on my left hand
the bruise—dark purple

holding in the pain
silence of sorrow
ashes spread on the ocean
settling in layers
palimpsest of lives
like maple leaves

      (How does death feel?)

impressions left on the sidewalk after
they've blown away
a raven on the roof that said
      Disconnect the phone

I turn on the gas
to make *Oyako Donburi*
tears come
while cutting up the onions—
isn't that the best gift?

I crack cold eggs
whip
and pour them over
boiling Napa and chicken broth
close the pot lid
turn off the gas
wait

      (Was I here before? Will I come back again?)

pour over bowl of rice
feed child—

Empty unmade bed—
a summer river where
I didn't want to see his body

Separation
One poet said
after his wife's funeral
he found a strand of her hair
on the pillow and wept

I made sukiyaki the day my dad died
I had to feed my children

Oxtail soup
That's what Daddy made—
suck out all the dead blood
and boil until broth turns milky—

When I leave
I want to leave beautifully

Mustard Flowers Falling

1.

a yellow cab stops in the dark
dark clouds cover half the moon
water is boiling in the rusty kettle

she smells like peppermint
the cat's eyes like a neon sign
outside the rainy window

you are reading a line in a poem
slowly
            slowly

petals of dried flowers
drop on your knees

a woman leaves
after brushing her teeth
with your old tooth brush

2.

with your old toothbrush
after brushing her teeth
a woman leaves

drop on your knees
petals of dried flowers

            slowly
slowly
you are reading a line in a poem

outside the rainy window
the cat's eyes like a neon sign
she smells like peppermint

water is boiling in the rusty kettle
dark clouds cover half the moon
a yellow cab stops in the dark

Dear Yeobo

When you say *ramen*
then I am ramen.

When you say *tea*
I am tea.

When you take off your clothes
I take off my clothes.

If I could leave my senses
I would be no trouble.

You don't give food
to the fish you've caught.

You no longer need to hold me—
please drink your tea.

Footnote:

Yeobo: a Korean term of endearment meaning "darling" or "honey"

Yang Kong Ju

Koreans called her
Yang kalbo
Yankee's whore

Korean men say
No thanks—
even though it's free

She started working at clubs
doing dishes
cleaning tables, mixing
drinks for soldiers
for tips

More tips to sit next to them
More tips to pour Jack Daniels for them
More tips to touch them there with tiny bare hands
More tips to say, *I like it*

Once nobody
now a swan

She speaks some English—
honee, Got dem it—
exhales Virginia Slims
smoke between whiskey
red virgin blood
polished finger nails

Her GI tongues her
neck, gropes her breasts
Stop it, she giggles

Lucky lucky seven
when she becomes
bride to white American

Her GI laces up
his boots. Hard as stone, she says

Marry me

GI tucks a dollar bill
in her lace black bra

Lucky Seven

1.
She comes back to Korea
with cases & cases of black market gold:
    Johnny Walker
    Marlboros
    M&Ms
    Vaseline
    Aspirin
    Ponds

Now she doesn't have to boil
in the kitchen
cook for her ill-tempered father
or overbearing brothers

Now, abusive mother smiles, gives the warmest
spot in *ohn dol bang*
She sits there and her sister brings food to her
She smokes and drinks American coffee
Her younger brother brings her a crystal ashtray

2.
She is not Korean
but alien
from a dark moon

She takes the whole family
to America
They bury her

Footnote:

ohn dol bang: related to *ondol*, the Chinese character for the Korean term *gudeul*, meaning "baked stones"; the ondol is an under-floor heating system which originated in ancient Korea.

Asian Woman

> *Isn't it about time Chosŏn women lived like humans?*
> —Na Hye-Sok

This is what you do with your life:

Take what your father gives you
care, food, shelter
Learn to be wife
cook, sew, maintain your household
Obey orders, serve your family, command
servants

This is what you do with your life:

Take what your husband gives you
care, food, shelter
Bury the jealousy of his concubines
be their big sister
Bear sons or you are useless
raise them to be fine young men
never take your eyes off them
Never tempt a lover

This is what you do with your life:

Take what your sons give you
care, food, shelter
Make your son's wives obey
Demand your son's wives bear sons

This is what you do with your life:

Teach your daughters
    to be like a song

three years deaf
    three years blind
        three years mute

teach them
    to be like you

Footnotes:

1.   In the epigraph above, *Chosŏn* refers to Korean.

2.   Na Hye-sok (1896–1948) was a pioneering Korean feminist writer and painter. As the first female professional painter in Korea, she created some of the country's earliest Western-style paintings. Also a poet, educator, and journalist, she became known as a feminist in the early 20th century with her strong criticisms of the marital institution (source: Wikipedia).

3.   See also "Rha Hye-Seok: Korea's Most Daring Feminist Artist: Discover the art and ideas of Korea's first professional female painter" in Google Arts & Culture:
    https://artsandculture.google.com/theme/NwLCYpagiV90JQ

✧

While Cleaning the Bellybutton

While cleaning my new baby's navel
with alcohol
I miss Mom
who birthed me through her bellybutton

When I was a child
I touched my Oma's navel
and asked,
How does the baby come out from here?

Oma looked at the wall
and answered,
Umm... the bellybutton grows big and opens—
then the baby comes out.

I gathered my girlfriends and whispered,
I know where the baby comes out!
     Where?
From the bellybutton.
     Really?
Really.

I really don't know why I still believe
this myth, even after giving birth myself.

After my mom gave birth to me
through her bellybutton, I gave birth
to my baby through my bellybutton—
and my daughter will give birth
the same way.

But where are you, Mom?
Didn't you promise me
if I have a baby,
you would help me raise it?
Aren't you supposed to be here
making seaweed soup for my birthday?

Where are you, Oma?
My tears, like the alcohol,
fall on my baby's bellybutton.

Look Back

1. "Oma, how did you come to America?"

my 14-year-old daughter asks.

The textbook answer or the truth?
"For better education, better opportunities,
and a better life," I say.

"Oma, it's so boring. All Asians in my class
have the same answers."

Yes, we want to run away from the truth.
We want to forget, not remember.
We want to protect—not to cause problems.

> We learn to pretend.
> Delete names.
> Disconnect.

I didn't want to look back.
My mother's open eyes
in her closed casket.

But, I have to write this story for me.

2. Paper Divorce

Rumors of war
when the Korean President
Park Chung-Hee got shot.

Mother wanted us to go
to America: strongest, richest
paradise of the world.

But, no tickets.
No lucky relative married to an American.

Paper divorce
was my parents' decision.
Of course, they didn't ask
our permission.

Best shot
for their children:
New paper mom in the States.

It happened secretly
of course
it was illegal,
but to survive, I learned
to pretend not to know.

3. Interview with an Immigration Officer

Only the children, four of us,
had to be interviewed.
My father worried
we wouldn't pass.

My sister and brothers sat
in silence.
It was always my duty
to perform.

Where is your mother?

(My mother made us breakfast this
morning, but it is not in the script.)

I put on a sad face.
"We didn't see our mom for two years.
We lost contact.
We hope to see her before
we go to America."

I lied with an innocent face,
letting my tears drop
as I gazed at his hands.

> *Where are you going to live?*

> (Is this how I learned to live in illusion?)

"We will go to Hawaii and live
with our father and a new mother."

> He is writing on a yellow pad.

> *What about your youngest sister?*

> (Do I have a younger sister? Oh, my father's
> love child.)

> *Why isn't she going with you?*

> (She is always a stumbling block.)

"She is too young to go.
She lives with our mother."

> (Another lie.)

> *What do you want to do in America?*

"To study hard and become a good person—"

He stamps the paper.
Have a good life in America.

Second Period

I am called to a little dark room,
windowless. Mrs. Lopez shows me
a picture book.

Khang, I say.

No, river, she says.

Liver, I say.

Not liver, it's river, she says.

That's what I said, river, river, river, khang—
It's a khang!

She shakes her head.
Look at my mouth, she says, *RRRRR*
VVVVVVVVVVVVVV

River.
River, I say.
Then shut my mouth.

✧

American Dream

Lunch time over,
the deli is like a cemetery.

I weigh salads on a scale,
punch numbers on the register:
12 hours a day standing
for my hungry stomach—

What about the dream
of America?
Don't dare to ask this question.

Once, waiting to be somebody
wore me out,
depleted my soul.

No more.
Invisible like a ghost,
obedient like a Sheltie,
deaf as a Grand Canyon rock—

Who am I to you,
America?

Shin-Mun Mother

your scent awakens milky dawn
always waiting for me by the door

all these years
ready to speak

I make a cup of coffee and open you
still warm

taking me back home
all the way around the world

I am speechless in this land
choked with fear into silence

you wind the thread
around my thumbs

quickly push the needle
releasing black blood

I can breathe
again

Author's Note:

When I was growing up in Korea, whenever we had a stomach ache, Grandmother or Mother or one of our aunts would wind our thumb with white cotton thread and push the sewing needle in to release black blood. When my aunt pushed her needle into my thumb, it was painful, but when I saw black blood coming out, I felt better and could breathe again. I don't know if modern medicine would approve, but it worked for us.

Confronting My Father's Mistress

1.
Ten years after he died
I phoned her.
I could finally call him
bastard
in English.

2.
Yeo bo say yo? she said (in Korean).

Can we talk? I asked
(in English).

Ung, she said. *I have no customers
now.*

I swallowed.
*How did you meet
my father?*

I heard the train passing—

Through a friend, she said.

Liar. I heard:
You were engaged.
Your fiancé was in the army.
You were a hairdresser
in our home town.
You knew
my father was a married man.
You met my father
at a night club.

*After that someone sent milk and
bread to my beauty shop every
morning.*

You came to our house, I said.
I was only seven.

3.
On children's day in May,
my father's mistress
dressed in strawberry with
a vanilla hat.
My mom served her
tea, in my dad's old socks,
gently tucked my father's ashtray
next to his folded pajamas.
Only the smell of his
Benson & Hedges
remained.

The neighbors watched
excited to see
blood
play their roles.

Your mother invited me.
She said, I am his wife.
These are his children.
You must stop.

You didn't, I said.

Now, I am a mother,
a wife,
a woman too.

How dare you.
You told my mother
she makes love to emptiness.

How can I forget my mother losing
her mind. A crazy
moaning animal.
I was fourteen.

Our daughter was born.
She needed her father beside her.

4.
My father robbed my older sister's
first name, *Jung.*
Gave it to *her*
child.
Half of my name
cut off for *her*
child.
It felt (I can't say it)…

5.
My daughter will be alone
when I die.

6.
You   stole   my dad.
You   stole   my name.
You   stole   my childhood.

7.
Too much silence.
I heard the howls of my mother's
mothers, their buried sorrows
and their thousands of years'
han.

I hung up the phone.

✧

The War Still Within

Tonight my tongue cuts galaxy
black bones be fire
a crying cello drifting
if I open my mouth
I will be sent to the Taklimakan
Desert a graveyard
silence of a thousand skulls
Endless black
Nothing can live
My eyes a flame
I never talk about the battleground
My secret burns there
My silence is your mouth
My skull the house of story
My jaw hinges
star-dirt
devastation in a capsule

White man said

> *No one listens to you*
> *No one sees*
> *Open your mouth*

I said

> *Go ahead*
> *Cut and burn my tongue*
> *You can't set fire to my secrets*
> *My other tongue*
> *will speak*

> *I carry my eyes, my bones*
> > *through this war*

✧

The Crying Game

[a persona poem, in noir style]

One November morning outside Saratoga Springs
over coffee at the Red Roof Inn you say
We're leaving for Florida
Vivid snapshots cross my mind
like race cars crashing on a track
No! my voice shakes into a laugh
shocked by my own answer
Hurricane fists, broken glass—
I catch the danger in your eyes

Later: *Eleven minutes, we're leaving*
and you slam the bathroom door
I grab your .38
from the nightstand drawer
where it lies next to Gideon's Bible
nudge the door open
Shaving cream all over your face
like a mug shot of Santa without the hat
in our reflection
I'm pointing the gun
at the back of your head
For a moment
we're young and silly again...

You think I'm pathetic
I give you a smile, then fire:
No more spaghetti sauce burning my skin
No more black eyes
No more 3 a.m. knife at my throat
No more broken nose after the football game
No more muffled screams

I didn't mean to shoot you
five times
but the gun only had five bullets

Heo Nanseolheon (1563–1589)

If women have *han* in their hearts—

> To be born a woman
> To be born in the Chosŏn Period
> To be the wife of a husband

—frost will come in May.

Father let me study poetry with my brothers
until I married Kim Song Lip and I put it aside.
Waiting for my faithless husband, Father said:

> *Write a poem.*

> *Ask yourself,*

> *Who am I?*

Footnote:

Heo Nanseolheon, born Heo Chohui, was a prominent Korean female poet of
the mid Chosŏn dynasty:
https://en.wikipedia.org/wiki/Heo_Nanseolheon

Mistranslation of Your Latest Letter

You signed
Yours truly,
The weight of language
races my heart beat.

Yeon-wonhan-dangshi ui

Yours truly
translates in Korean:
I am yours like the river holding
down stones, yours like the body
to bone. I am yours like hinges
on a brownstone's front door.
I am always yours,
no white sheets between
my soul and your skin—

Is that right?
You could have fooled me.

✧

Mother Tongue

Sophistication isn't damn good to drink.
So why don't you untie my tongue
like you undress me in the dark, don't
let my ego ruin our night, don't
scan betrayal in your mind—life's not so bad
if you don't pay attention.
Reaching out in the night, I don't know
what I'm trying to grasp.
When the sound of a trumpet wraps my body,
I want to speak in my mother tongue.
I don't apologize, *Sorry, sorry*
English isn't my first language...
Yes, I smell like garlic—don't kiss me,
I had kimchi—you smell, too, like scorched lamb
and limburger; let's just love each other.

Like June Snow

405 North to Manhattan
You play "One Fine Day" for me on the phone
Too much noise in your film studio
The siren sound of ambulance
The tea spills
A new pink scar
The phone disconnects
like   heaven   and earth

It could be our last
conversation. The weight of love
the weight of pain
Are   the   same
I lie to myself: I am fine
I am fine   without you

You here   You there
doesn't matter anymore

You   didn't   call
last   Friday   I pan fried 12 dozen
dumplings   baked 12 dozen chocolate cookies
all burnt   the taste of our first kiss

I left you   I leave you   over and over
but   I can never leave you

Your voice wraps me in sable
in raindrops   in fire
I fall asleep on the tile,
you calling   my name
Words could fall from a satellite
from November's sky
turn light on my eyes

I send email: *Sorry—I can't talk tomorrow or Friday*
Will try one fine day

Our love melts   like June snow
I will dry your voice
press it like a gingko leaf
tuck it in my suitcase

✧

The Cost of Breath

Talk about the wood
stacked high in the living room
what it costs
to breathe in my home—
raw wood, oak
so long and thick—
a dead elephant stretched wall to wall

He said to acclimate takes time
and more money—heartwood
slow to open, to respire—
one week
     became a month
         became a year

I couldn't breathe
A pile of planks
unusable, forlorn
it had to go

I want to speak my mind
instead of smile
Nice girls don't speak
their minds or
question men—

How dear it is
to breathe

Soft as Rock

I should want nothing
your kiss, touch, embrace
not even the smile that says
I know you
I should not want
to speak—my mouth should be a stone
on this pillow beside you

my mouth is open
with longing, hungry
to taste you

Even stones yearn
flowers grow
between them
glowing, the deep tree roots
break apart with life
sweetness pushing through like song

At Tara Station in Dublin

I stopped time
I came to this island, over the dark-blue Irish sea,
where the sun does not often rise.

Like Rimbaud, the young poet, who had gone
to Africa, who put his hands in the pockets
of his short coat and
pulled down his hat and
carried an old empty bag,

I myself left to find my Africa.
I ended up at Tara Station in Dublin,
near Irish people who look like the innocents
in children's books,
and with a group of travelers holding their tickets,
on which their destinations are written.

An abundance of different station names...
I tried hard to find the one that smelled most
like the sea, as I searched the board from A to Z.
I missed the last train and was locked into Tara Station.

At the pub nearby, I sat drinking
an Irish coffee, while looking at sad Dublin city,
getting wet with the night rain.

A sweet-looking girl came up to me and asked,
not in Gaelic but in fluent English:
"Love! I am a hungry angel of the street.
Get me a McDonald's hamburger and a cup of coffee,
and tell me a story of your star,
the land where you came from, please."

✧

End Notes

More than seven million Koreans now live in diaspora, in 170 countries, and the first of several waves of Korean international migration began in 1860. As described in the introduction to "Diasporic Art and Korean Identity,"

> "…artists are particularly able to captivate audiences and innovate ways of articulating the multiple aspects of the everyday condition of diasporic existence *in situ.…*"

> Korea University and University of California, Berkeley: *Cross-Currents: East Asian History and Culture Review* 29:1-14 (Dec. 2018):

> https://cross-currents.berkeley.edu/sites/default/files/
> e-journal/articles/Cross-Currents%2029%20-
> %20H.%20Son%20and%20J.%20Rhee_3.pdf

Living and writing from two cultures, hers [Tanya Ko Hong's] is a unique, authentic, and courageous voice. Her poetry creates a voice for multiple generations of Korean women, especially the "comfort women" who were silenced during and after WWII.

> —AROHO, 30 September 2014
> (A Room of Her Own Foundation for Women)

About the Author

Tanya Ko Hong (Hyonhye) is a poet, translator, and cultural-curator who champions bilingual poetry and poets. Born and raised in Suk Su Dong, South Korea, she immigrated to the U.S. at the age of eighteen. She is the author of five books: *The War Still Within* (KYSO Flash Press, 2019); *Mother to Myself,* a collection of poems in Korean (Purunsasang Press, 2015); *Yellow Flowers on a Rainy Day* (Oma Books of the Pacific, 2003); *Mother's Diary of Generation 1.5* (Qumran Publishing, 2002); and *Generation 1.5* (Korea: Esprit Books, 1993).

Her poetry appears in *Rattle, Beloit Poetry Journal, Entropy, Cultural Weekly, WSQ: Women's Studies Quarterly* (published by The Feminist Press), *Lunch Ticket, great weather for MEDIA, Califragile,* the *Choson Ilbo, The Korea Times, Korea Central Daily News*, and the *Aeolian Harp Series Anthology*, among others.

Tanya was one of two writers to receive the inaugural Yun Dong-ju Korean-American Literature Award in 2018. Her work was also a finalist in the 2018 Frontier Digital Chapbook Contest, and has been nominated for a Pushcart Prize. In 2015, her segmented poem *Comfort Woman* received an honorable mention from the Women's National Book Association. Her poems have been translated into Korean, Japanese, and Albanian. In 2015 and 2018, she became the first person to translate and publish Arthur Sze's poems in Korean.

Tanya serves on the Board of Directors of the AROHO Foundation (A Room of Her Own), is pursuing a Ph.D. in Mythological Studies at Pacifica Graduate Institute, and holds an MFA degree from Antioch University in Los Angeles and a Sociology degree from Biola University. She lives in southern California.

Author's website: http://www.tanyakohong.com

Credits: First Publications

The author gratefully acknowledges the publications listed below in which many of the poems in this collection first appeared, some of which were in slightly different versions.

Beloit Poetry Journal (Volume 65, Number 1, Fall 2014): two sections from the segmented poem *Comfort Woman*: "1943, Shanghai, China" and "1946, Chinju, Korea"

Berkeley Korean Literature Society (2016): "Mustard Flowers Falling" (reprinted in 2018 by the Los Angeles Poet Society)

Birds Fall Silent in the Mechanical Sea (great weather for MEDIA, 2019; anthology): "The Crying Game"

Cultural Weekly (June 2015): "Look Back"

Entropy Magazine (Dis·Articulations): "The War Still Within" published 30 November 2017 in a slightly different version and with the title "The War Still Inside You"; poem was written by Tanya Ko Hong using words generated by Terry Wolverton through fevered writing, and later reprinted as "The War Still Inside Me" in *Aeolian Harp Series*: *Anthology of Poetry Folios* (Volume 4, 2018).

FRE&D: "Mother Tongue" (Volume 1, May 2014); and "Shin-Mun Mother" (Vol. 2, Spring 2015), published as "Shin-Moon Mother"

Generation 1.5 (Korea: Esprit Books, 1993) by Tanya Hyonhye Ko: "At Tara Station in Dublin"

great weather for MEDIA: See *Birds Fall Silent in the Mechanical Sea* above, and *The Other Side of Violet* below.

Palos Verdes Library District Anthology (2015): "Waiting"

Paris Press, Spiraling Poetry: "Grandmother Talks of Camptowns"; "Heo Nanseolheon (1563–1589)"; and "Oxtail Soup" (2015)

Rattle (#46, Winter 2014): "Dear Yeobo" and
Rattle (#59, Spring 2018): "A Blonde Whispers Korean In My Ear"

The Feminist Press: See "*WSQ: Women's Studies Quarterly*" below.

The Long-Islander *Huntington Weekly* newspaper, "Walt's Corner" (June 7–13, 2018): "*Bo go ship uh* (I miss you)"

The Other Side of Violet (anthology; great weather for MEDIA, 2017): "Lucky Seven"

They Write by Night, YouTube series on film noir and poets, Suzanne Lummis narrating (2 June 2018): "The Crying Game": https://www.youtube.com/watch?v=d5DfHHHyMsU

Two Hawks Quarterly (Winter 2013): "Second Period" and "Gacela of Moonshine"

Unmasked: Women Write About Sex and Intimacy After Fifty (Weeping Willow Books, 2017): "Soft as Rock" (published in a slightly different version, under the title "Denied")

WSQ: Women's Studies Quarterly, The Feminist Press (Volume 47, Numbers 1 & 2, Spring/Summer 2019): "Confronting My Father's Mistress" and "The Cost of Breath"

Yellow Flowers on a Rainy Day (Oma Books of the Pacific, 2003) by Tanya Hyonhye Ko: "The Way to Cross the Desert" and "While Cleaning the Bellybutton"

✧

Alphabetical List of Poems

About the Cover Photo

Compiled by Clare MacQueen

The front-cover image is a cropped and tinted version of the black-and-white photograph reproduced herein on the title page, from the U.S. National Archives.* Photo caption in the Archives Catalog refers to "Japanese Prisoners" that were taken by the Chinese 8th Army, but the image actually shows four Korean "comfort women." They were among the few survivors of sexual slavery forced upon an estimated 200,000–300,000 women by the Japanese Imperial Army during World War II. The original photograph was shot by Charles H. Hatfield (U.S. Army 164th Signal Photo Company) on September third, 1944, after the Chinese troops had captured the women from the Japanese.

The young pregnant woman in the foreground was Park Young-shim (Pak Yong-sim, 1921–2006). In December 2000, fifty-six years after that haunting photograph was taken, she testified at The Women's International War Crimes Tribunal in Tokyo, about the atrocities she and others suffered during WWII.

To learn more about her, see "Some Concluding Thoughts" in the article by Philip Charrier, Associate Professor of History at the University of Regina: "'Comfort Women' at Songshan, China, September 1944: A Picture Story" (September 18, 2017):

https://www.uregina.ca/arts/perspectives/philip-charrier.html

For recent news about the image, see "Original photographs of comfort women made public for first time: Seoul exhibits photos to celebrate centennial anniversary of Mar. 1 Movement," an article by Kim Hyang-mi in *The Hankyoreh* (19 February 2019):

http://english.hani.co.kr/arti/english_edition/e_international/882785.html

---

* Footnote:

The vast majority of digital images in the U.S. National Archives Catalog are in the public domain, including the photograph on the front cover of this book; therefore, no written permission and no fees are required to use the image. Its Catalog record, SC-230147 (Original Field Number CBI-44-29969), states specifically under "Details" that access and use are unrestricted (link retrieved on 27 August 2019):

https://catalog.archives.gov/id/142663321

Further Readings:

1. "Comfort stations" was the euphemism used by the Japanese Imperial Army (JIA) for the military brothels it established in 1932. Operations were hugely expanded during WWII as the JIA forcibly "recruited" hundreds of thousands of women, the majority of whom were girls between the ages of 14 and 19, in Japanese-occupied territories to provide so-called "comfort" for troops at the front lines. As per Wikipedia's extensive entry on "comfort women," it's estimated that more than half were Korean.

For more information, see "The Brutal History of Japan's 'Comfort Women'" by Erin Blakemore, in *HISTORY* (updated 21 July 2019):

https://www.history.com/news/comfort-women-japan-military-brothels-korea

2. The first of three major waves of Korean immigration to the United States began in 1903, with the arrival of 102 Koreans in Honolulu on 13 January. Although many were not farmers but came from urban seaports, the men soon found work as contracted laborers for pineapple and sugar plantations in the Hawaiian islands. Two years later, more than 7,000 Koreans had arrived in the U.S. before Japan halted emigration from Korea in 1905, thus ending the first wave.

For more information, see "History of Korean Immigration to America, from 1903 to Present" (Boston Korean Diaspora Project):

http://sites.bu.edu/koreandiaspora/issues/history-of-korean-immigration-to-america-from-1903-to-present/

About the Editor

Clare MacQueen served as webmaster and copy editor for 18 issues of *Serving House Journal* from its launch online in 2010 to its retirement in 2018. She co-edited *Steve Kowit: This Unspeakably Marvelous Life* (Serving House Books, 2015). She's also co-editor, webmaster, and publisher of *KYSO Flash*, the online literary journal and micro-press that she founded in 2014 to celebrate a smorgasbord of short-form writings and visual art. Via KYSO Flash Press, she has custom-designed and produced 18 books, including anthologies and collections for writers and artists whose works have been published in *KYSO Flash* online. Her own essays, reviews, stories, and poems have appeared in, among others, *New Flash Fiction Review, Ribbons, Serving House Journal, Skylark,* and the anthologies *Best New Writing 2007* (Hopewell Publications) and *Winter Tales II: Women on the Art of Aging* (Serving House Books, 2012).

www.kysoflash.com

an online literary journal &
a micro-press of printed books

Knock-Your-Socks-Off Art and Literature

CPSIA information can be obtained
at www.ICGtesting.com
Printed in the USA
BVHW060835260120
570361BV00002B/2